YGNACIO VALLEY

DESERT MAMMALS

A TRUE BOOK

by
Elaine Landau

Children's Press®
A Division of Scholastic Inc.

New York Toronto London Auckland Sydney
Mexico City New Delhi Hong Kong
Danbury, Connecticut

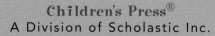

For Michael—
our oasis in the desert

Reading Consultant
Linda Cornwell
Learning Resource Consultant
Indiana Department of
Education

Subject Consultant
Kathy Carlstead, Ph.D.
National Zoological Park
Smithsonian Institution

Addaxes have long,
spiral horns.

Library of Congress Cataloging-in-Publication Data

Landau, Elaine.
    Desert mammals / by Elaine Landau.
        p.   cm. — (A true book)
    Includes bibliographical references and index.
    Summary: Describes such animals as camels and how they adapt to
life in various deserts around the world.
    ISBN 0-516-20038-0 (lib. bdg.)   ISBN 0-516-26097-9 (pbk.)
    1. Desert animals—Juvenile literature. [1. Desert animals.] I. Title.
II. Series.
QL116.L35   1996
591.909'54—dc20   96-3891
                                                                        CIP
                                                                        AC

Contents

Though very little rain falls in the desert, many animals live in this harsh environment.

Deserts

Think of a desert. Did you imagine miles of sand and rock beneath a scorching sun? All deserts get less than 10 inches (25 centimeters) of rain a year. But not all deserts are wastelands. Some have wide areas of plant growth, and some have hills and mountains. A number of animals also live in deserts.

Deserts cover about one-fifth of the earth's land surface. There are deserts in North America, South America, Africa, Asia, and Australia. The deserts of the world differ in size, temperature, and weather conditions. But all are home to a variety of mammals. Mammals are animals with backbones and with more highly developed

Desert plants provide food for animals.

brains than other animals. They are also the only animals that nurse their young. This book introduces some interesting desert mammals and shows how they survive the desert's harsh conditions.

Canada

NORTH AMERICA

United States

Kansas

Arizona Oklahoma
New
Mexico

Mexico

CENTRAL
AMERICA

SOUTH
AMERICA

Sahar
Deser

E

AFI

Pallid bat colonies are
found in desert areas
in Mexico and the
southwestern
United States
as well as up
through parts
of Canada. They
may also be found
in southern Kansas
and northern
Oklahoma.

Antelope
jackrabbits
are found in
desert areas
of New Mexico
and Arizona.

Kangaroo rats
are found in
desert areas in
the southwestern
United States
and Mexico.

N

W   E

S

ANTAF

ROPE

A S I A

Gobi
Desert

Middle
East

Wild camels exist in Asia in the Gobi Desert. Domestic camels can be found in Africa, Asia, the Middle East, and Australia.

CA

Addaxes are found in parts of northern Africa's Sahara Desert.

AUSTRALIA

TICA

Camels

If you were asked to name a desert animal, would you say the camel? Camels are mentioned in many songs, stories, and films about deserts. A camel's most unusual feature is the hump on its back. The hump is actually a lump of fat that

The camel is an interesting desert mammal (above). A Bactrian camel (inset) has two humps.

provides the camel with energy when food is scarce.

There are two types of camels—the Arabian, or one-humped camel, and the Bactrian, or two-humped camel. Both are well suited to the desert. The camel has long, thick eyelashes that stop wind-blown sand from getting in its eyes. And its nostrils close tight to keep out sand. The camel's bushy

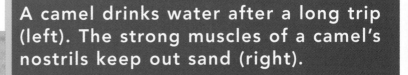

A camel drinks water after a long trip (left). The strong muscles of a camel's nostrils keep out sand (right).

eyebrows are also useful. They shade its eyes from the sun.

Camels can go without water for weeks, especially if they can feed on dew-dampened plants or desert fruits. A camel can lose one-fourth of its body weight in water without any distress.

Camels do not store water in their humps, but their bodies conserve water in other ways. Unlike humans, camels do not sweat much. Instead, their body temperature tends to rise slowly during the day and drop at night.

Camels have been used by desert people since early times. Even today, they carry heavy loads through the desert and help with other chores.

Children are curious about a camel at the zoo.

There are no longer any one-humped camels in the wild—all are domesticated. However, some small herds of two-humped camels still roam free. Today, these animals are in danger of dying out, so they are protected by law.

Kangaroo Rats

The kangaroo rat is a tiny
desert animal that jumps like
a kangaroo. Like a kangaroo,
it has a long tail and powerful
hind legs that help it leap long
distances. While only about
2 inches (5 cm) tall, a kangaroo
rat can cover as much as 2 feet
(0.6 meters) in a single jump.

The long tail of a kangaroo rat helps it stay balanced as it hops across the desert.

Like many other small desert animals, kangaroo rats spend the hot daylight hours in cool underground burrows. At night, when the temperature drops, they come out to look for food. They eat mostly

A kangaroo rat sleeps in its burrow (right). Kangaroo rats store food in their burrows (left). They pack their cheeks with seeds to carry to their burrows.

seed grains and the green parts of plants.

Kangaroo rats thrive in the desert because they can live without water. Their bodies make their own water from

18

the food they eat and the air they breathe. In laboratory experiments, kangaroo rats have survived for more than fifty days on only dry seeds. At that point their bodies were still about 65 percent water.

Kangaroo rats feed on green parts of desert plants.

The kangaroo rat's body
also conserves or saves water.
These animals do not pant or
sweat, and they release only
a small amount of water in
their urine. Therefore,
kangaroo rats play an

A kangaroo rat
leaves its tracks
in the sand.

Coyotes (above) and bobcats (right) are predators of the kangaroo rat.

important role in the desert's food chain. They are a valuable source of moist meat for rattlesnakes, coyotes, foxes, bobcats, and other animals that eat them.

A pallid bat flies through the air.

Pallid Bats

After dark in the desert, you might see a light-colored creature gliding through the air. It swoops down to snatch a small lizard or insect for its dinner. At first you may think it's a large bird, but it's a bat!

The pallid bat lives in the desert, in colonies of 15 to

A colony of bats gathers in a cave. Scientists tag the bats to study their behavior (above). Pallid bats have long ears (right).

100 bats. It measures 2 to 3 inches (5 to 8 cm) long with a 1- to 2-inch (2.5- to 5-cm) tail. The pallid bat has yellowish beige fur on top and white underparts. It has

unusually large ears and a small horseshoe-shaped ridge on its muzzle.

During the day, the pallid bat rests out of the sun on overhanging cliffs, in hollow trees, or within deep cracks in desert rocks. Twice each night

A pallid bat resting

it goes out to look for food. After descending on its prey, the pallid bat sometimes eats its prey on the ground. These bats eat crickets, beetles, grasshoppers, and scorpions.

Pallid bats are highly social and use a variety of calls to communicate with one another. Baby bats are born in June, following the mating season. Usually, the female gives birth to twins. The baby bats open their eyes when

A pallid bat eats a scorpion.

they are five days old and
learn to fly in about six weeks.
   While pallid bats may look
frightening, these animals
actually help humans with pest
control. They eat a number of
bothersome insects.

An antelope jack rabbit is actually
a hare, not a rabbit.

Antelope Jack Rabbits

When is a rabbit not really a rabbit? When it's an antelope jack rabbit!

The antelope jack rabbit may look like a rabbit, but it is actually a hare. Hares are larger than rabbits, and they have longer ears and bigger feet. Even when they are

A baby antelope jack rabbit

born, these animals look different. Rabbits are born hairless with their eyes tightly shut. Hares come into the world open-eyed and furry.

The antelope jack rabbit is about 2 feet (0.6 m) long with 7- to 8-inch (18- to 20-cm) long ears. Its coat is grayish brown on top and mostly white underneath. Its long

Excess body heat is released through an antelope jack rabbit's ears.

An antelope jack rabbit rests in the shade.

ears help this desert mammal survive. When it becomes too warm, the antelope jack rabbit can release its body heat through its ears. Yet, during cold desert nights, its ears help it stay warm. The antelope jack rabbit holds body heat by keeping its ears down and close to its body.

During the hottest part of the day, antelope jack rabbits rest in shallow holes in the ground or beneath a shady plant. In the late afternoon and at night, they feed on desert grasses, prickly pears, and other plants.

During the mating season, male antelope jack rabbits often fight over females. The males rise up on their hind legs and grunt and groan while throwing punches at one another. Bites and kicks often follow until one animal gives up. The winner gets the female.

Antelope jack rabbits are well adapted to desert life.

Addaxes can withstand harsh desert heat.

Addaxes

The addax, a broadly built, short-tailed antelope, is well adapted to its desert habitat. An addax can stand extremely high temperatures. And its wide hoofs help it travel easily across broad stretches of sand.

Small addax herds of ten to twenty animals are always in

A herd of addaxes

search of grazing land. These animals are so sensitive to weather conditions that they can detect a thunderstorm miles away. The herd then heads in that direction, because a heavy rainfall can turn a desert green. Other times, their wanderings may take these animals far from a water source. However, like many desert animals, an addax can go for a long time without drinking water.

An addax and her young graze on desert grasses (left). An addax easily moves across desert sand with its wide hoofs (right).

The addax stands about 3.5 feet (1 m) high. Its color blends in with its desert surroundings. In summer, it is beige on top with white lower parts. In winter, as the

An addax has a darker coat in winter.

The addax has long and unusual horns.

landscape changes, the addax's coat becomes darker and longer.

Perhaps this animal's most outstanding feature is its long, twisted, spiral horns. These unusual horns make the animal look as though it stepped out of a storybook. Male addaxes fight each other with their horns to determine which is strongest and most dominant.

Sadly, the addax is powerless against its worst enemy—humans. Armed hunters chase these animals in automobiles

The number of addaxes has fallen over the years. Care must be taken to preserve these graceful desert mammals.

and gun them down. The addax is unable to outrun a car and becomes an easy target for the hunter's bullet. Today, the addax is in danger of becoming extinct.

To Find Out More

Here are more places to learn about desert mammals:

Books

Arnold, Caroline. **Camel.** Morrow Junior Books, 1992.

Arnold, Caroline. **Watching Desert Wildlife.** Carolrhoda, 1994.

Brandenberg, Jim. **Sand and Fog: Adventures in Southern Africa.** Walker & Company, 1994.

Dewey, Jennifer. **A Night and Day in the Desert.** Little, Brown, 1991.

Lerner, Carol. **Cactus.** Morrow Junior Books, 1992.

Sayre, April Pulley. **Desert.** Twenty-first Century Books, 1994.

Organizations

National Park Service
Office of Public Inquiries
P.O. Box 37127
Washington, DC 20013
(202) 208-4747
http://www.nps.gov

NPS/Western Region
National Park Service
600 Harrison Street
Suite 600
San Francisco, CA 94107
(415) 744-3929

Sierra Club
730 Polk Street
San Francisco, CA 94109
(415) 776-2211
http://www.sierraclub.org/

**Smithsonian: National
Zoological Park**
3000 block of
Connecticut Avenue NW
Washington, DC 20008
(202) 673-4800
http://www.si.sgi.com/
perspect.afafam/afazoo.
htm

Interactive

Life in the Desert.
ZooGuide's Library.
This CD-ROM includes
photos and video of the
many fascinating desert
mammals. Ages 7+

Africa Trail. MECC.
Explore the vast continent
of Africa and learn about
its interesting animals.
Ages 7+

Dromedary Camel
*http://aztec.asu.edu/
phxzoo/camel_dr.html*
Discover all about the
dromedary camel and
its desert life.

Mexican Gray Wolf
*http://aztec.asu.edu/
phxzoo/wolfmexn.html*
Learn about this
mysterious creature
of Mexico.

LlamaWeb
*http://www.webcom.com/
%7Edegraham/About/
Camelids.html*
This online site includes
facts and interesting
stories about llamas,
camels, alpacas,
and vicunas.

Important Words

adapt to change to make suitable

burrow hole in the ground made by an animal for shelter

conserve to save

detect to discover or become aware of

domesticated tame

extinct no longer existing

habitat an animal's environment

herd a group of animals

muzzel an animal's outwardly extending jaw and nose

prey an animal hunted by another for food

spiral winding

thrive to do well

Index

Meet the Author

Elaine Landau worked as a newspaper reporter, children's book editor, and youth services librarian before becoming a full-time writer. She has written more than ninety books for young people.

When redecorating their home, Ms. Landau and her family filled it with desert plants. But they had to draw the line at animals. Although everyone thought a camel would be terrific— they felt the animal might be somewhat cramped in the family rec room.